THE PICTURE LIFE OF
STEVIE WONDER

THE PICTURE LIFE OF

BY AUDREY EDWARDS
AND GARY WOHL

30345000530942

FRANKLIN WATTS
NEW YORK | LONDON | 1977

Photographs courtesy of:

Larry Yelen: p. 2; Johnson Publishing Co., Ebony Magazine: pp. 6, 9, 10, 13, 14, 17, 18, 21, 22, 25; Globe Photos: p. 26; Motown: p. 27; Newsweek-Robert R. McElroy: p. 33; Newsweek-Lester Sloan: pp. 34, 35; Bob Gruen: p. 37; William R. Eastabrook: p. 44; Ed Galluci: p. 45; Bill Pierce: p. 48.

Library of Congress Cataloging in Publication Data

Edwards, Audrey.
    The picture life of Stevie Wonder.

    (Picture life books)
    SUMMARY: A biography of a young, blind musician who had his first hit record at the age of thirteen.
    1. Wonder, Stevie — Juvenile literature.
2. Rock musicians — United States — Biography. — Juvenile literature. [1. Wonder, Stevie.
2. Musicians. 3. Afro-Americans — Biography]
I. Wohl, Gary, joint author. II. Title.
    ML3930.W65E4 784'.092'4 [B] [92] 76-47566
ISBN 0-531-01271-9

Copyright© 1977 by Franklin Watts, Inc.
All rights reserved
Printed in the United States of America
5 4 3 2 1

# THE PICTURE LIFE OF
STEVIE WONDER

The young, blind boy on the stage threw his head back. "You are the sunshine of my life," he began to sing in a deep voice. The words of the song rose and filled the air. The people in the audience sat quietly and listened to the love song.

They were listening to Stevie Wonder sing. He stood with his arms stretched out. It looked as if he were trying to give his words to the people.

Stevie also began playing before people when he was very young. Here he belts out a song like a real pro.

Stevie Wonder has been playing and singing music all of his life. He was born blind. Some people say he was given the gift of music in place of the gift of sight. It is a gift he has used well.

He is one of the few musicians who is very good at many things. He is a fine singer, a great songwriter, and a master at playing many instruments.

Stevie spent most of his time playing and singing music. Here he plays the electric piano.

Stevie began playing music almost before he began to talk. At age two, he was using a spoon to beat out drum sounds on a tin pan. He played along with the music on the radio.

By age four, Stevie began playing the piano. Then he learned to play a harmonica his uncle had given him. At the age of nine, Stevie could play the piano, the drums, and the bongos, too.

Stevie, with his mother,
brothers, and sister.
He is playing for them
on the bongos.

He did not let the fact that he was blind keep him from playing music, or leading a normal life. Stevie was born Steveland Morris on May 13, 1950, in Saginaw, Michigan. He was one of six brothers and sisters. Stevie spent most of his early life in Detroit, Michigan, where he played like other children and often got into trouble like other children.

Stevie had many friends in Detroit, where he grew up. Even though he was blind, Stevie would climb trees with the other children.

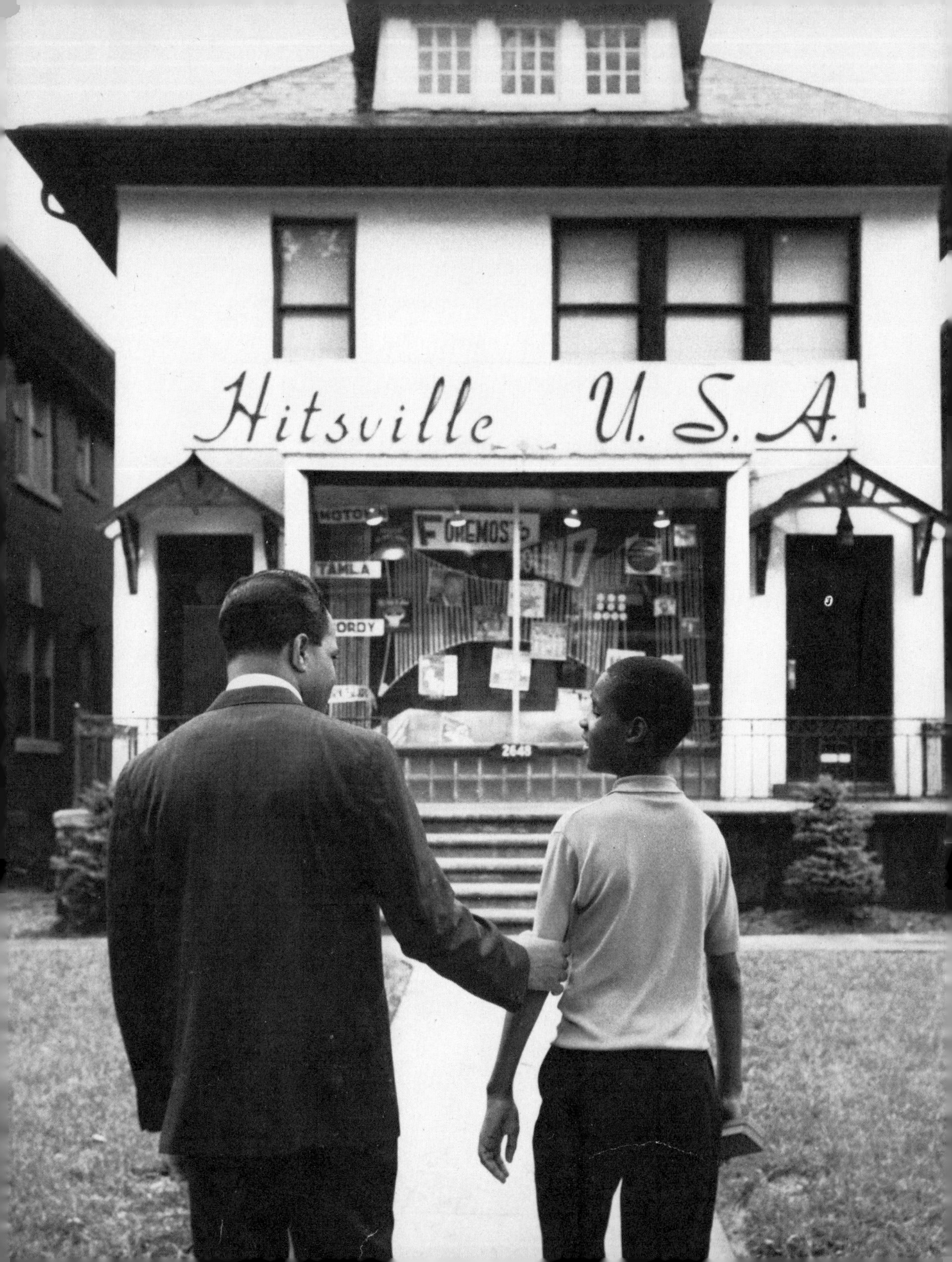
Hitsville U.S.A.
TAMLA
2648

When Stevie was ten years old, a singer with a group called the Miracles heard about how talented he was. The singer took Stevie to a black recording company to sing and play his songs.

The name of the company was Hitsville, U.S.A. The name would later be changed to Motown. And Motown would record some of the most popular black singers in the country.

Berry Gordy, Jr., the head of the Motown recording company, helped Stevie get started. At first the company was called Hitsville, U.S.A.

Berry Gordy, Jr., the president of Motown, liked Stevie's music very much. It had a lively, fun beat. He agreed to record Stevie's songs. Stevie signed a contract with the company. Now he would be paid for his songs. At age ten, Stevie had become a recording artist! Berry Gordy even changed Stevie's name to Stevie Wonder.

When he was only ten, Stevie was using the recording equipment in Motown's studio.

Now that he recorded for Motown, Stevie traveled a lot. He traveled with other Motown singers around the country. He was part of the Motown Revue. It was very exciting. He traveled with such stars as the Temptations, the Supremes, Marvin Gaye, and the Miracles. He also met many people who came to see and hear him, the "boy wonder."

Stevie stops for a moment outside the Regal Theatre in Chicago. In April, 1963, he performed there with the other stars in the Motown Revue.

In 1963, when he was 13, Stevie recorded his first big hit for Motown. The song was called "Fingertips." It had a wild, fast beat that Stevie played with the harmonica. Teenagers everywhere loved to dance to "Fingertips." And the song sold over a million records! Stevie Wonder was on his way to becoming a star.

A crowd of young fans lines up to get Stevie's autograph. He was always a big hit when he traveled with the Motown Revue.

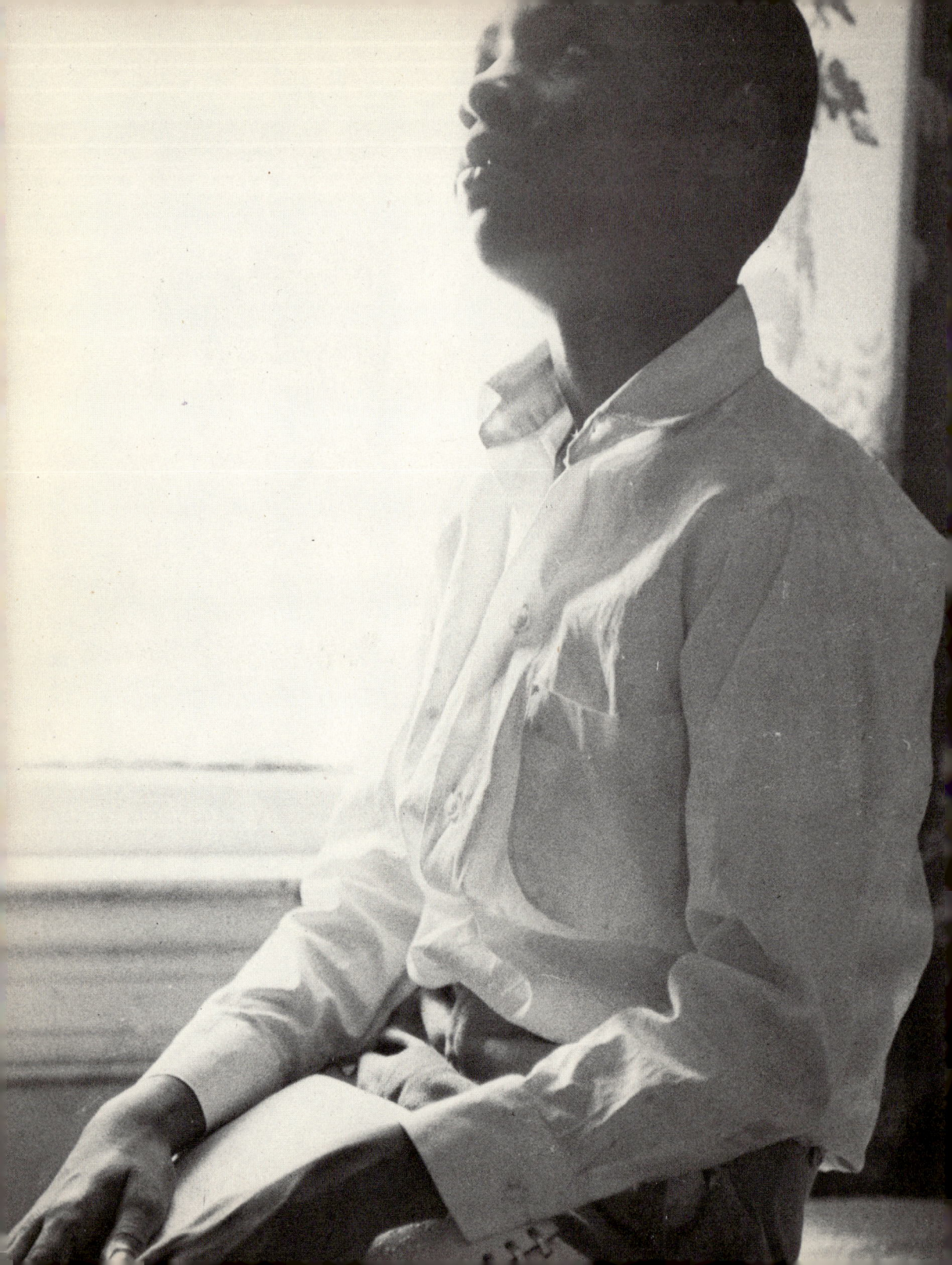

But Stevie was still very young, and had to go to school like other teenagers. Because he traveled often, he had his own teacher. Stevie studied for two weeks out of every month. The other two weeks he spent traveling on the road.

When he wasn't appearing on stage, Stevie studied his school lessons. Here he "reads" in braille. Words written in braille have raised dots. Blind people read by using their fingers to feel the dots.

Stevie continued to turn out hit records for Motown. Songs such as "Uptight," "Blowin' in the Wind," "A Place in the Sun," and "Yester-Me, Yester-You, Yesterday" all became number one on the record charts. It seemed that every song Stevie touched turned to gold.

While he was still a teenager, Stevie began singing and playing his songs in some very fancy places. In 1969, at age 19, he gave his own concert at New York's Philharmonic Hall. In 1970, he appeared at a famous supper club in New York called the Copacabana.

Stevie signs one of the many albums he recorded for Motown when he was still very young. One of them was a tribute to "Uncle" Ray Charles, another blind piano player.

THE JAZZ SOUL
OF LITTLE STEVIE
TRIBUTE To UNCLE RAY
LITTLE STEVIE WONDER

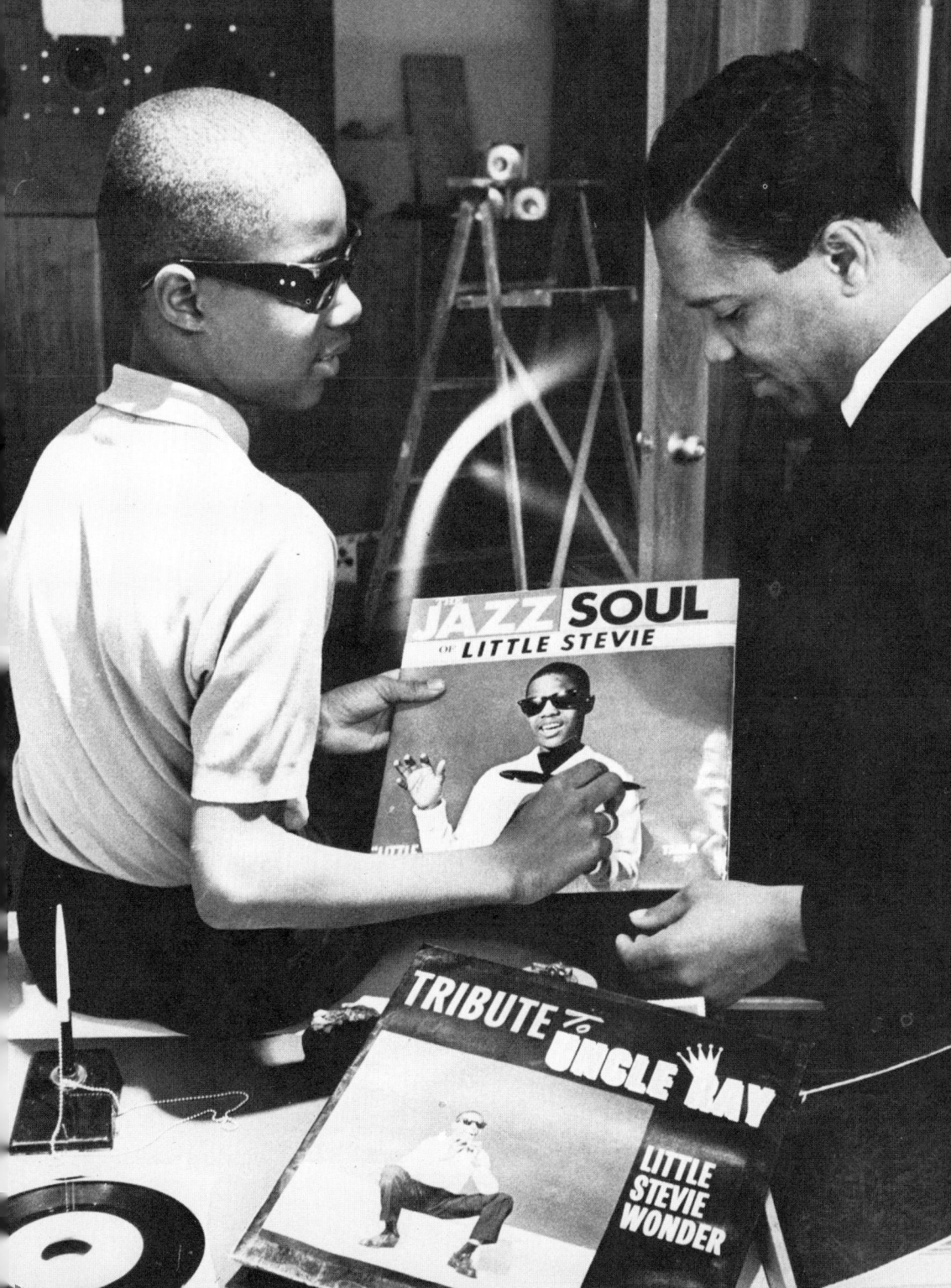

Stevie with another young singer, Bobby Rydell.

People loved to see Stevie's act. He would often start singing and then run to the piano and play. Then he would jump up and start dancing. He had as much fun as the people did who were watching him!

When he was 20, Stevie made his first album. He wrote most of the songs himself. His mother, Mrs. Lula Hardaway, helped him with some of them. The album was called "Signed, Sealed and Delivered." It became a big hit. The title song became a gold record. That meant it sold over one million copies.

Stevie talks with Supreme Court Justice Earl Warren after singing at the Annual NAACP Freedom Fund Dinner in 1970.

Stevie enjoyed his success. But he began to grow tired of the songs he was doing for Motown. Then he made "Music of My Mind." The album was different from anything Stevie had ever done. For the first time, Stevie used a "synthesizer" to make his music. A synthesizer can make any sound.

On this album, Stevie was beginning to sing and play about the things that he felt. It was his biggest hit yet.

Stevie at twenty years old.

In 1972, Stevie went on a tour around the country with the Rolling Stones. They were a very popular white "rock and roll" group. Before his trip with the Rolling Stones, most of the people who listened to Stevie's music were black. By appearing with the Rolling Stones, Stevie gave more white audiences a chance to hear his music. They loved it. He was now popular with both blacks and whites.

When Stevie appeared in 1972 with the Rolling Stones, Madison Square Garden was sold out. Here he and Mick Jagger, leader of the Rolling Stones, sing a song together.

On the trip, Stevie sang songs from his new record "Talking Book." He also showed people his new backup group, called Wonderlove. The group had ten musicians and three singers. People in the audience screamed and cheered for Stevie and his new group.

In 1973, Stevie made another album. This one was called "Innervisions." It was about Stevie's search to find meaning in his life and in the world. His songs showed an interest in people and the things that were happening to them.

Stevie takes time out from his work to talk to a group of fifth graders. The youngsters are doing a film story about him for television.

Stevie plays many of the instruments on his albums and sings all of the songs. The fancy equipment helps give his music a different sound.

Even though Stevie was blind, he could "see" better than many people. He wanted to share with people the things he "saw" through his music.

But on August 6, 1973, Stevie was in a terrible car accident. He was being driven to a concert when a truck ahead of his car suddenly stopped. The truck was filled with logs that fell out and smashed into the car window. Stevie was hit on the head and knocked out. He was taken to a hospital, where he lay near death for almost two weeks!

It took many months for Stevie to get well. He wondered if he would ever be able to play music again. He did not know it, but he would play better than ever.

At Christmas time in 1974, Stevie sold out Madison Square Garden again. He invited other recording stars to come on stage with him. From left to right are Roberta Flack, Stevie, and Sly of Sly and the Family Stone.

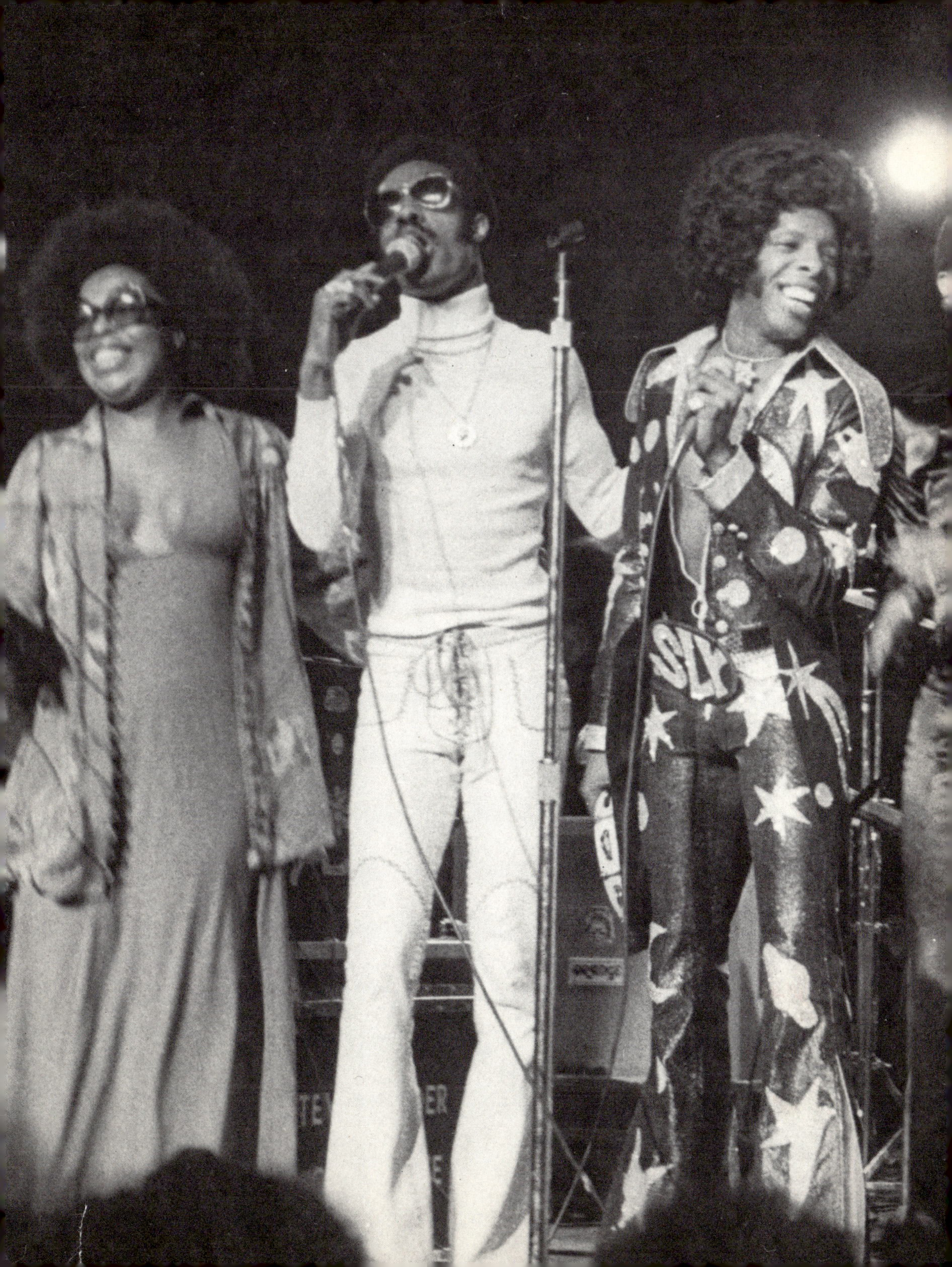
SLY

Stevie with Helen Reddy.
They both won Grammys in 1974.

In 1974, the recording industry honored Stevie's music. He was given five Grammy awards that year for the "Innervisions" album. Grammy's are given every year for the best music.

During the year, Stevie also sang in places all over the country, and in parts of Europe. He even went as far as Japan. Everywhere he went, people came to see and hear him. "Stevie! Stevie!" they cried. "Give us another song! Sing one more song!"

A year after his accident, Stevie made an album called "Fulfillingness' First Finale." This time he sang about the wrongs he saw in the world. And he sang about the need to give love. Stevie's accident had made life more special to him. He was glad to be alive. He wanted to use his music to teach people to love.

Stevie, dressed in one of his mod suits, listens closely to someone.

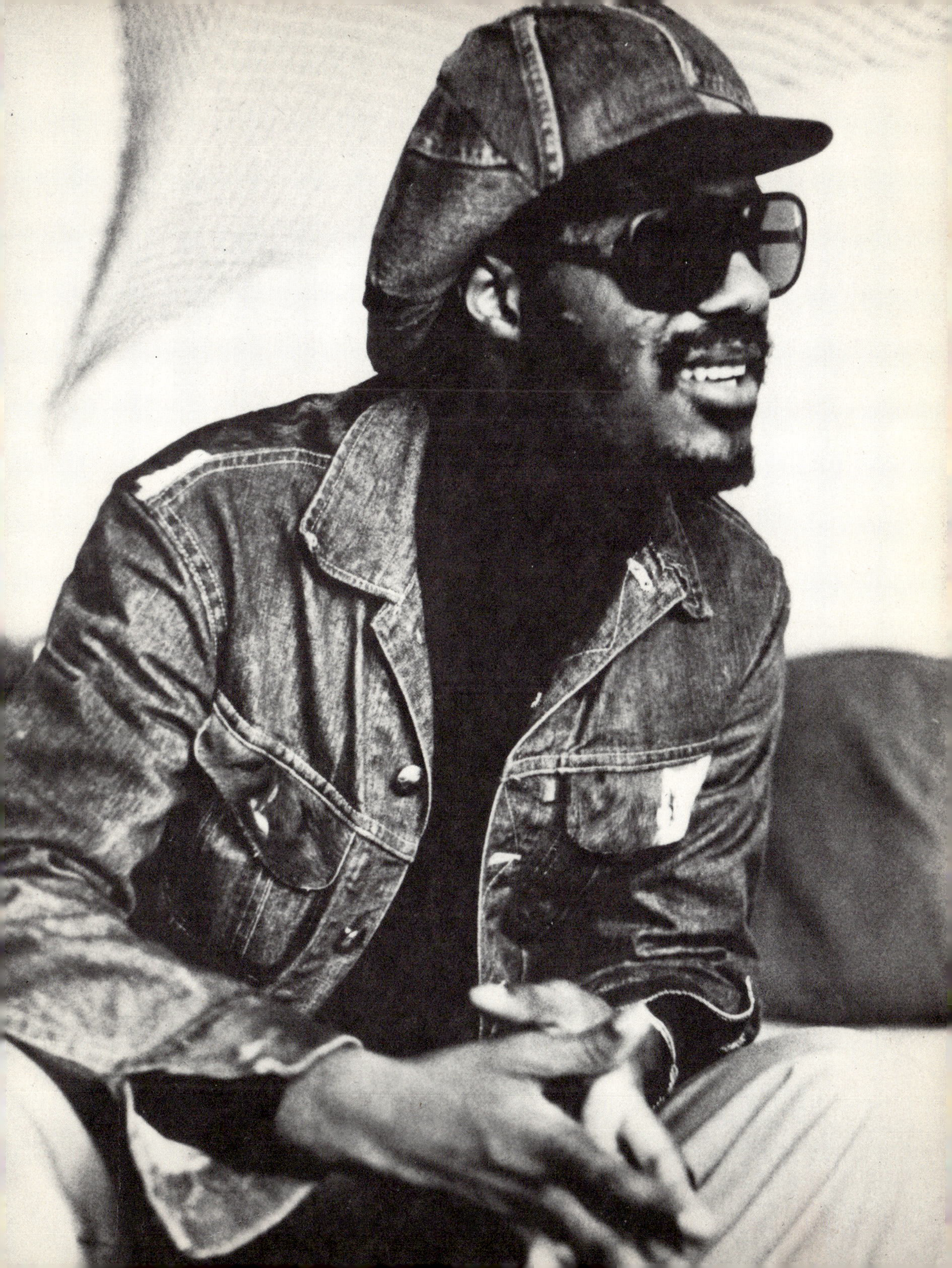

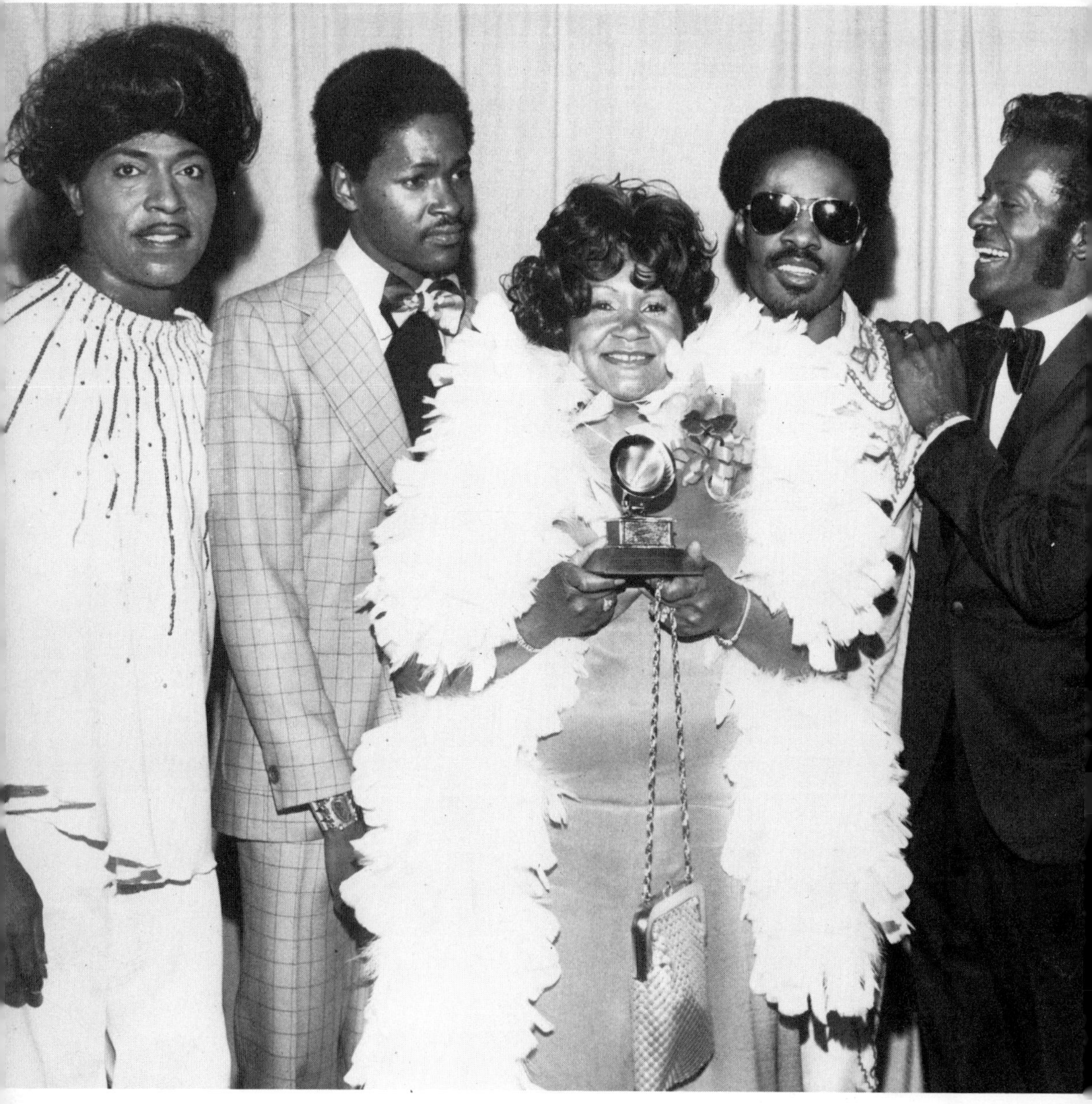

The recording industry honored Stevie again in 1975. He got five more Grammys for his "Fulfillingness' First Finale" album.

Stevie's mother holds one of the five Grammy awards her son received in 1974 for "Innvervisions." From left to right are singer Little Richard, Stevie's brother, Calvin Hardaway, his mother, Stevie, and singer Chuck Berry.

The year 1975 was a big year for Stevie in another way, too. On April 7, 1975, Stevie became the proud father of a baby daughter. Stevie and the baby's mother, Yolanda Simmons, named their child Aisha Zakia. It is an African name that means "life and intelligence."

Stevie gives a loving hug to Yolanda Simmons.

Stevie in the garden of his
townhouse in Manhattan, New York City.

Stevie Wonder has given the world more than just his music. He has given more than $80,000 to charities and schools to help people. In May, 1975, he was a special guest on Human Kindness Day in Washington, D.C. On that day, he played and sang for over 250,000 people for free.

With each new record, Stevie's music showed more growth. Each one was better and more popular than the last one. The success of his next album, released in 1976, was hard to believe. In just one week it sold over two million copies!

Over 250,000 people crowded the streets of Washington, D.C., to hear Stevie sing on Human Kindness Day.

Music is Stevie's first love. And he puts everything he has into it. "You see," he says, "music is my way of giving back love." His love is as big as his talent.

Grover from "Sesame Street" seems to love Stevie's songs as much as real people do.